MORE

LET'S CELEBRATE

written by Ruth Esrig Brinn
illustrated by Katherine Janus Kahn

*To my husband Chester,
who shares all my celebrations*

KAR-BEN COPIES, INC. ROCKVILLE, MD

Library of Congress Cataloging in Publication Data
Brinn, Ruth Esrig.
  More let's celebrate.

  Summary: Provides instructions for 57 Shabbat and Jewish holiday crafts and suggests related activities.
  1. Jewish crafts—Juvenile literature. 2. Fasts and feasts—Judaism—Juvenile literature. [1. Jewish crafts. 2. Holiday decorations. 3. Handicraft. 4. Fasts and feasts—Judaism] I. Kahn, Katherine, ill. II. Title.
BM729.H35B75 1984   745.5   84.25104
ISBN 0-930494-38-5

Published by KAR-BEN COPIES, INC., Rockville, MD
Printed in the United States of America

CONTENTS

PESACH

Forsythia Flowers, Colorful Kippah, Wine Tray, Matzah Tray, Seder Pillow, Four Cup Counter, Haggadah Bookmark, "No Hands" Seder Game, Moses in the Basket

YOM HA'ATZMAUT

Walk-a-thon Backsack, Birthday Fun for Israel, Fruity Milkshake

LAG B'OMER

Golf Course, Shoe Puppet, Star Pinwheel, Picnic Pocket, Colored Bubbles

SHAVUOT

Shavuot Paper Cut, Basket for Shavuot Greens, Confirmation Cap

A NOTE TO THE BOYS AND GIRLS WHO WILL USE THIS BOOK

MORE LET'S CELEBRATE will show you how to make crafts for the Jewish holidays. All of them are fun and easy and will make holiday time very special for you.

The crafts are made from odds and ends you find around the house. Ask your family to help you save old magazines, packing material, tissue paper, leftover wallpaper and fabric, empty spice jars, paper towel rolls, egg cartons, juice cans, spools and the like.

Turn the pages to see what you can create. When you know what you want to make, find a good place to work, and gather all the supplies. You may not need a grown-up's help, but make sure you tell someone what you will be doing and where you will be working.

Keep this book in a special place so that you can look at it often. Make something to celebrate each of the Jewish holidays.

SHABBAT

COUNTER FOR SHABBAT

What You Need:

Paper plate
Colored markers
Construction paper
Scissors, stapler
Plastic straw
Brad fastener
Yarn

What You Do:

1. Draw lines dividing the plate in half and then in half again. Draw lines dividing three of the triangles in half. You will have six thin triangles and one fat one.

2. Decorate the fat triangle with Shabbat objects and write SHABBAT SHALOM on it. Decorate and number the other triangles from 1-6.

3. Cut the straw in half and attach it to the center of the plate to make a pointer. Staple a yarn hanger to the top of the plate.

ONE, TWO, THREE, FOUR, FIVE, SIX...SHABBAT!

glue

What You Need:

Colored construction paper
Colored tissue paper
Glue, scissors, markers

TRY THIS TOO: Make a new ring of Shabbat flowers for each season: fall, winter, spring and summer.

What You Do:

1. Cut a long thin strip of colored paper for the ring.

2. Cut several stems from green paper and glue them to the ring. The bottom of each stem should reach the bottom of the strip for support.

3. Cut flowers in different shapes and colors. Decorate with markers and tissue paper. Glue them to the stems.

4. Glue the edges of the strip together to make a ring.

FLOWERS HELP MAKE SHABBAT BEAUTIFUL

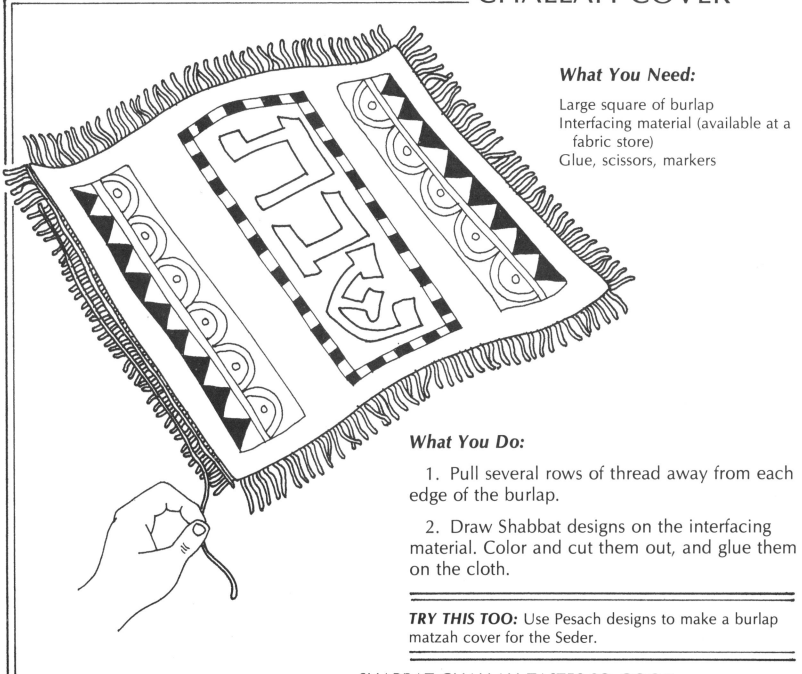

What You Need:

Large square of burlap
Interfacing material (available at a
    fabric store)
Glue, scissors, markers

What You Do:

1. Pull several rows of thread away from each edge of the burlap.

2. Draw Shabbat designs on the interfacing material. Color and cut them out, and glue them on the cloth.

TRY THIS TOO: Use Pesach designs to make a burlap matzah cover for the Seder.

SALT SHAKER FOR SHABBAT

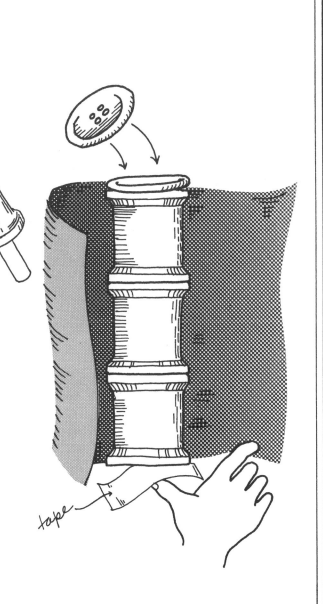

What You Need:

3 empty spools
Silver foil
Pencil or straw
Button
Glue, tape
Salt

What You Do:

1. Glue the spools together in a stack. Push a straw or pencil through the holes to keep them straight while the glue is drying.

2. Glue a button over the top opening.

3. Turn over and fill with salt. Tape the bottom opening so the salt won't spill. Wrap foil around the spools.

tape

SAY THE BLESSING AND SPRINKLE SALT ON YOUR SHABBAT CHALLAH

What You Need:

Paper plate
Pencil, colored markers
Scissors

What You Do:

1. In the center of the paper plate, draw and color a picture of the Shabbat table. Don't forget to include:

Candles
Cup of wine
Two loaves of challah covered by a pretty
 cloth
Shabbat flowers

2. With your scissors, carefully punch a hole in an empty section of the plate, and cut out the Shabbat shapes. Be careful not to cut the rim of the plate.

3. Fold over the rim to make the Shabbat picture stand.

MAKE DIFFERENT PICTURE STANDS FOR THE HOLIDAYS

SHINE-THROUGH KIDDUSH CUP

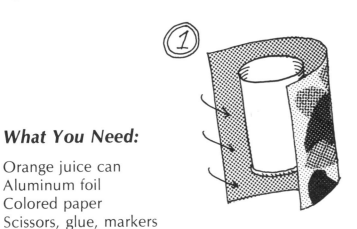

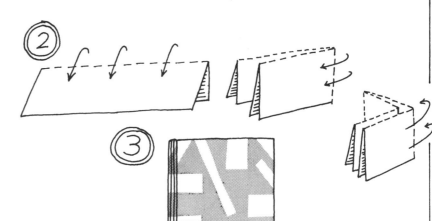

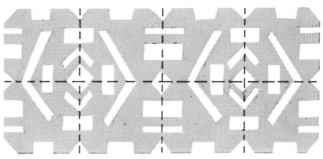

What You Need:

Orange juice can
Aluminum foil
Colored paper
Scissors, glue, markers

What You Do:

1. Cut a piece of foil large enough to cover the can and tuck in the edges. Make a scribble design on the foil with different colors. Wrinkle up the foil and then smooth it out. Cover the can with the foil, tucking in the edges.

2. Cut a piece of colored paper that will fit around the can exactly. Fold it in half lengthwise. Then fold it in half the other way twice.

3. Cut shapes from the corners and from each side. Open the paper carefully. Roll it around the can and glue the edges together.

TRY THIS TOO: Use a larger can to make a shine-through vase for Shabbat flowers or a pretty cup for Elijah to use at the Seder.

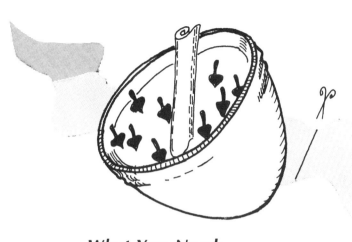

What You Need:

Plastic L'Eggs® box
Spices (whole cloves, cinnamon stick pieces)
Piece of nylon hose
Rubber band
Colored construction and tissue paper
Glue

What You Do:

1. Fill the bottom half of the "egg" with spices. Stretch a piece of nylon hose over the top. Use a rubber band to hold it tight. Glue a strip of colored paper over the rubber band. Decorate with colored tissue paper balls.

2. Cut out three stars and glue them to the cover. Keep your spice box covered so the spices will stay fresh.

THREE STARS IN THE SKY MEANS THE END OF SHABBAT. HAVE A GOOD WEEK!

ROSH HASHANAH

YOM KIPPUR

SHANAH TOVAH MAILBAG

fold

What You Do:

1. Cut out a large rectangle from the paper bag. Fold it in half and unfold it.

2. On each side, cut out a narrow strip from the bottom of the rectangle to the middle fold.

3. Fold the rectangle in half again. Fold over the ends of the larger section and glue them over the smaller section.

4. Cut a piece of yarn long enough to go over your shoulder. Staple it to the bag to form a handle.

5. Decorate the mailbag with shanah tovah symbols.

What You Need:

Large paper bag
Yarn
Crayons or colored markers
Scissors, glue, stapler

14

NOW YOU CAN BE A SHANAH TOVAH MAIL CARRIER!

MOSAIC SHANAH TOVAH

What You Need:

Colored tissue paper
Colored construction paper rectangle
Glue, scissors

What You Do:

1. Fold the rectangle of paper into thirds. Unfold. Fold the bottom third back underneath the middle section.

2. Draw a shofar, an apple, or another Rosh Hashanah symbol in the center of the middle section. Do not let it reach the edges. Punch a hole in the center of your drawing, and cut out the shape from the bottom and middle sections at the same time.

3. Turn the card over and unfold. Paste strips of colored tissue paper to cover all the cut-out space in the middle section. Put glue on the edges of the bottom section and fold it up over the middle section.

4. Now write a New Year message on the card.

TRY THIS TOO: Draw designs on a square of aluminum foil with colored markers. Crumple it and then flatten it out. Instead of the tissue paper, glue the foil over the cut-out section of your design.

HAVE A HAPPY NEW YEAR

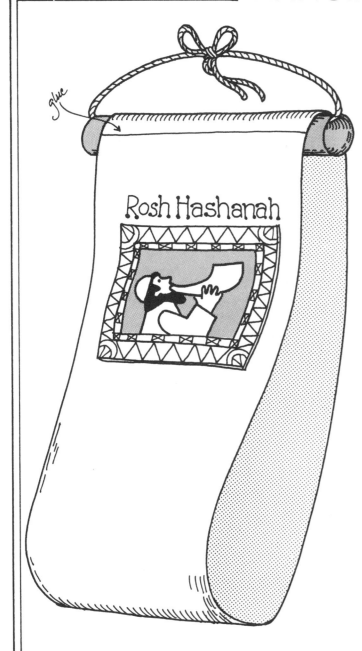

What You Need:

Large cardboard roll
Yarn
Long piece of shelf
 paper
Drawing paper
Scissors, glue, markers

What You Do:

1. Overlap the ends of the shelf paper and glue them together. Hang the paper over a cardboard roll. Push a piece of yarn through the roll and tie the ends together to make a hanger.

2. On a separate sheet of paper, draw a picture about Rosh Hashanah. You may choose to draw the table with candles, wine, challah, apples and honey...or the chazan blowing the shofar...or whatever you wish.

3. Glue the picture onto the shelf paper. Use a colored marker to draw a frame around the picture.

4. As each new holiday comes, add another picture to your album. Add more shelf paper if you need to make it longer.

WHICH HOLIDAY DO YOU LIKE BEST?

MAKE YOUR OWN RAISINS

The challah for Rosh Hashanah looks different—it's round! And some people like it with dark, plump raisins.

What You Need:

Paper towel
Seedless grapes

What You Do:

1. Put a paper towel on a sunny window sill. Put loose grapes on the towel.

2. Then...WAIT! The grapes will change a little every day. The warm sunshine will dry them out, and they will get more and more wrinkled until one day they will become... RAISINS!

Add some raisins to your challah dough, or mix some with nuts for a holiday snack.

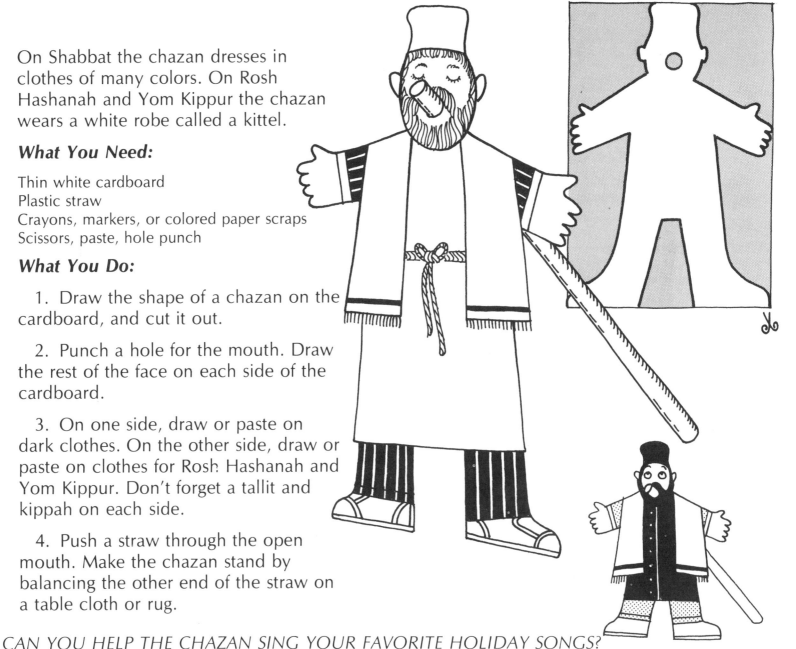

On Shabbat the chazan dresses in clothes of many colors. On Rosh Hashanah and Yom Kippur the chazan wears a white robe called a kittel.

What You Need:

Thin white cardboard
Plastic straw
Crayons, markers, or colored paper scraps
Scissors, paste, hole punch

What You Do:

1. Draw the shape of a chazan on the cardboard, and cut it out.

2. Punch a hole for the mouth. Draw the rest of the face on each side of the cardboard.

3. On one side, draw or paste on dark clothes. On the other side, draw or paste on clothes for Rosh Hashanah and Yom Kippur. Don't forget a tallit and kippah on each side.

4. Push a straw through the open mouth. Make the chazan stand by balancing the other end of the straw on a table cloth or rug.

18 *CAN YOU HELP THE CHAZAN SING YOUR FAVORITE HOLIDAY SONGS?*

SUKKOT

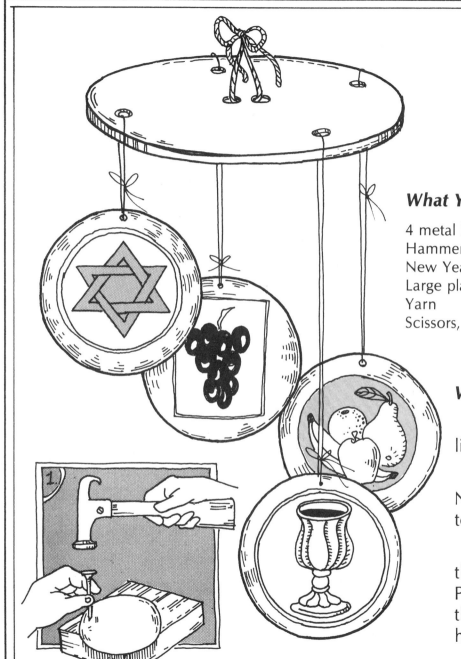

What You Need:

4 metal lids from juice cans (with rounded edges)
Hammer, thick nail
New Year cards or pictures from magazines
Large plastic lid
Yarn
Scissors, pencil, glue

What You Do:

1. Punch a hole near the edge of each lid. Tie a piece of yarn to each one.

2. Draw and cut out eight circles from New Year cards or magazines. Glue one to each side of each lid.

3. Punch four holes around the edge of the plastic lid. Tie the circles to the lid. Punch two more holes in the middle of the plastic lid, and tie a yarn handle to hang the mobile.

THE WIND WILL HELP MAKE MUSIC IN YOUR SUKKAH

A FRIENDLY SUKKAH BEE

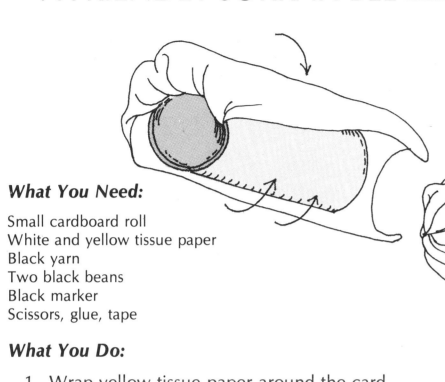

head

wing

What You Need:

Small cardboard roll
White and yellow tissue paper
Black yarn
Two black beans
Black marker
Scissors, glue, tape

What You Do:

1. Wrap yellow tissue paper around the cardboard roll and tuck in the ends. Draw black bee stripes around the roll.

2. Make a yellow tissue ball for the head and push it into one end of the roll. Glue two beans for eyes and black yarn for feelers.

3. Cut wings from white tissue paper and glue or tape them on. Tape six short pieces of black yarn for legs.

4. Fasten a long piece of yarn to the bee's body and hang it in the sukkah.

THIS FRIENDLY BEE WON'T STING

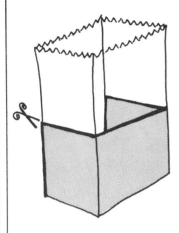

What You Need:

Large paper grocery bag
Colored paper
Yarn
Glue, scissors, markers

What You Do:

1. Cut off the bottom of the bag. Cut out one of the sides to form a sukkah with three walls and a floor.

2. Cut thin strips of green and brown paper and paste them across the top to form branches and leaves. Cut out colorful fruits and vegetables and fasten them to the walls and roof of the sukkah.

3. Draw pictures on the walls with markers.

22

FRUIT BOX

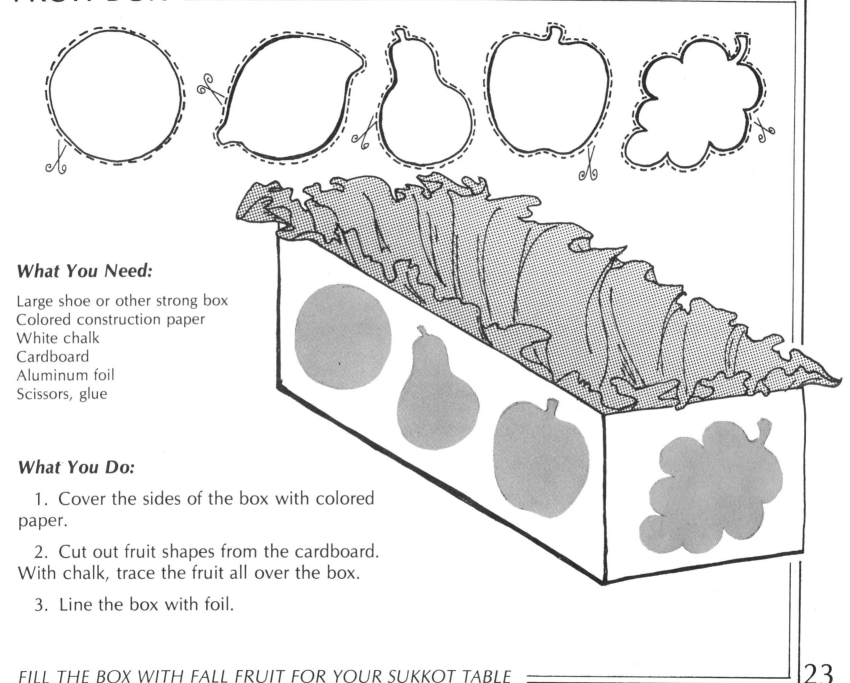

What You Need:

Large shoe or other strong box
Colored construction paper
White chalk
Cardboard
Aluminum foil
Scissors, glue

What You Do:

1. Cover the sides of the box with colored paper.

2. Cut out fruit shapes from the cardboard. With chalk, trace the fruit all over the box.

3. Line the box with foil.

FILL THE BOX WITH FALL FRUIT FOR YOUR SUKKOT TABLE

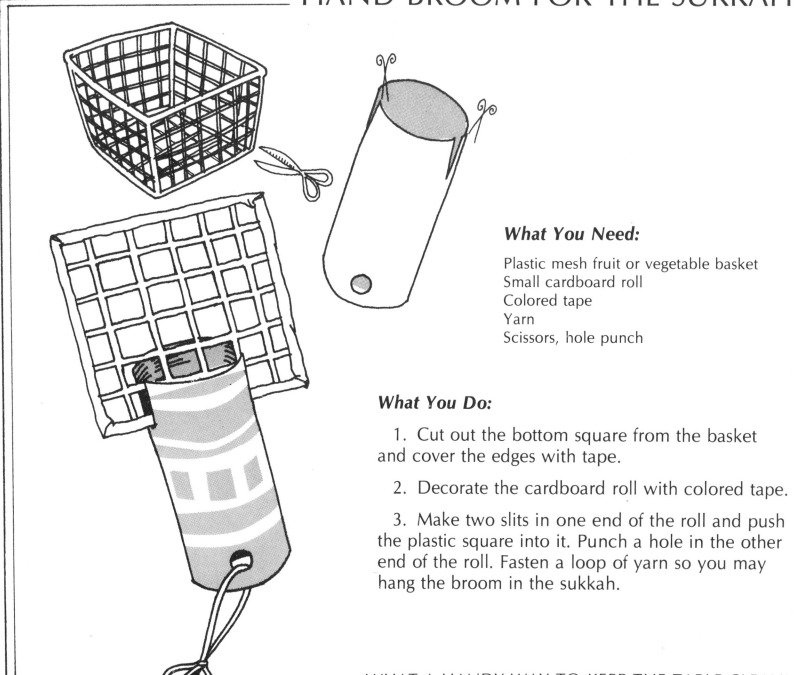

What You Need:

Plastic mesh fruit or vegetable basket
Small cardboard roll
Colored tape
Yarn
Scissors, hole punch

What You Do:

1. Cut out the bottom square from the basket and cover the edges with tape.

2. Decorate the cardboard roll with colored tape.

3. Make two slits in one end of the roll and push the plastic square into it. Punch a hole in the other end of the roll. Fasten a loop of yarn so you may hang the broom in the sukkah.

WHAT A HANDY WAY TO KEEP THE TABLE CLEAN!

TORAH MOBILE

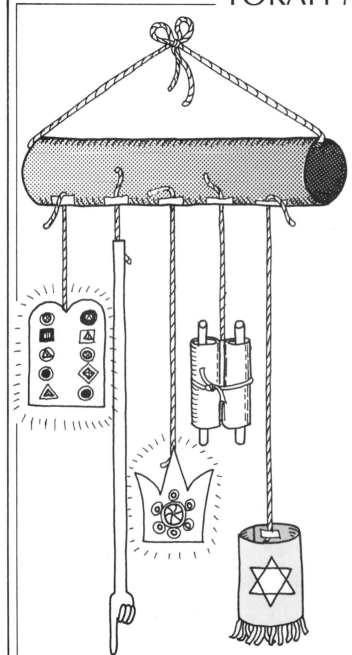

What You Need:

Large cardboard roll
Colored paper, aluminum foil
Cardboard
Yarn, colorful fabric
Drinking straw
Tape, stapler, scissors
Wire twister
Paint and paintbrush

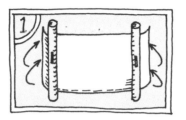

What You Do:

1. Torah scroll: Cut the straw in half. Staple each half to the ends of a narrow strip of paper. Roll the scroll and fasten with a wire twister.

2. Torah cover: Make a cylinder from a rectangle of fabric. Decorate with fringe.

3. Yad: Draw a hand with a pointing finger on a piece of cardboard. Cut it out and decorate.

4. Breast plate: Draw the shape of the two tablets of the Ten Commandments. Cut it out and cover with foil. Decorate with make-believe jewels.

5. Crown: Draw a crown shape on cardboard, cut out, and decorate.

6. Paint the cardboard roll. Tape or staple a piece of yarn to each object and tape the other ends to the cardboard roll. Make each piece of yarn a different length.

7. Push a long piece of yarn through the roll and tie the ends together.

HANG THE TORAH MOBILE FOR EVERYONE TO SEE

נס גדול היה שם

CHANUKAH

a great miracle happened there

FINGER FUN

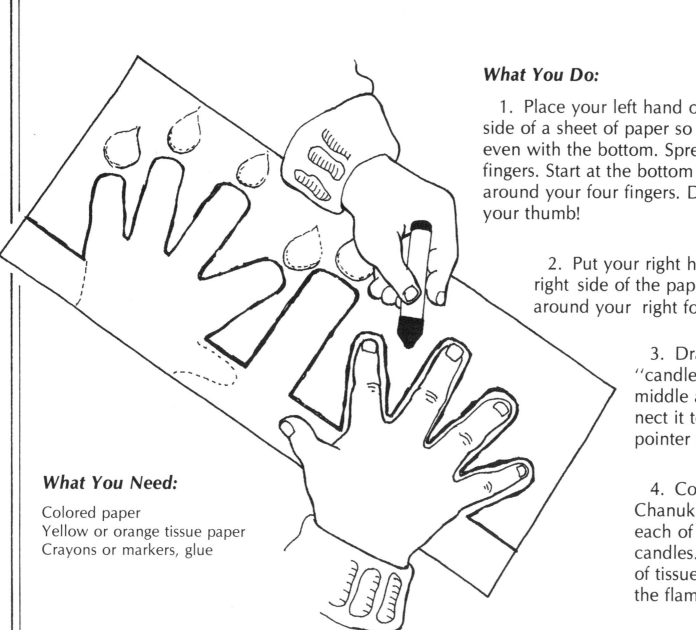

What You Do:

1. Place your left hand on the left side of a sheet of paper so your wrist is even with the bottom. Spread your fingers. Start at the bottom and trace around your four fingers. Don't trace your thumb!

2. Put your right hand on the right side of the paper and trace around your right four fingers.

3. Draw a large "candle" in the middle and connect it to each pointer finger.

4. Color the Chanukiyah and each of the candles. Glue bits of tissue paper for the flames.

What You Need:

Colored paper
Yellow or orange tissue paper
Crayons or markers, glue

DREIDEL MOBILE

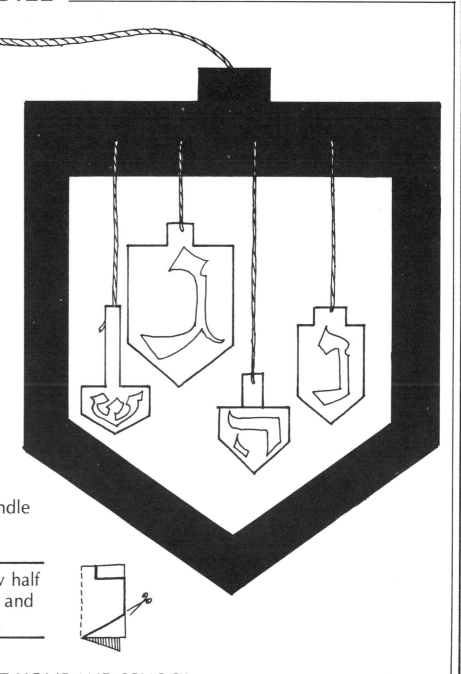

What You Need:

White shirt cardboard
Colored construction paper
Thread or thin yarn
Scissors, glue, markers

What You Do:

1. Draw and cut out a large dreidel shape from the cardboard. Draw a smaller dreidel shape inside the big one. Punch a hole in the center and cut out the inside dreidel.

2. Cut four tiny dreidels from colored paper. Cut four pieces of yarn or thread. Glue one end to each tiny dreidel and the other end to the big dreidel.

3. Glue a long piece of yarn to the handle of the large dreidel to hang.

Hint: Fold your paper in half and draw half a dreidel along the fold. Cut out, unfold, and you have a whole dreidel.

What You Need:

Glass table leg coaster (from hardware or variety
   store)
Felt
Picture from greeting card, magazine, or photograph
Glue, scissors, pencil

What You Do:

1. Choose a picture you like or draw one
of your own. Place the coaster over your picture, trace around it, and cut it out. Now
trace the coaster on the felt and cut it out.

2. Put glue around the edge of the coaster
and gently place it on top of the picture. Glue
the felt circle to the bottom of the paper
weight.

SCIENCE FUN

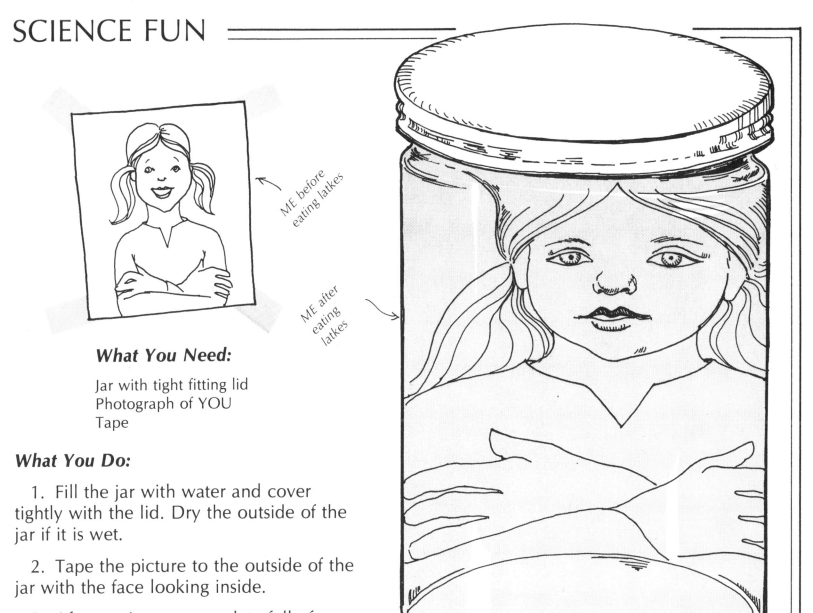

ME before eating latkes

ME after eating latkes

What You Need:

Jar with tight fitting lid
Photograph of YOU
Tape

What You Do:

1. Fill the jar with water and cover tightly with the lid. Dry the outside of the jar if it is wet.

2. Tape the picture to the outside of the jar with the face looking inside.

3. After you've eaten a plate full of crispy, crunchy Chanukah latkes, look at your picture through the water!

SEE HOW FULL YOU LOOK!

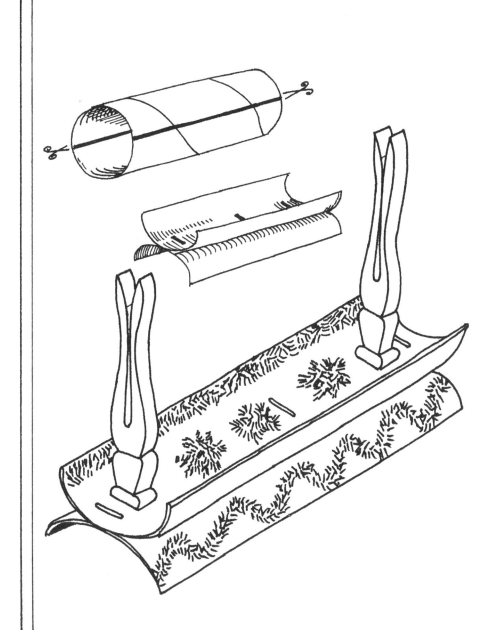

What You Need:

Small cardboard roll
2 wooden clothespins (without springs)
Salt
Colored chalk
Scissors, glue, stapler
Paint and paintbrush

What You Do:

1. Cut the cardboard roll in half the long way. Staple the curved ends back to back.

2. Glue the heads of the clothespins along the inside of the roll. When the glue is dry, paint the clothespins and base.

3. Rub colored chalk on the salt to make colored sparkles. Make a design on the holder with glue and sprinkle the colored salt on it. Shake off the extra salt. Sprinkle and shake until the design is just the way you like it.

YOUR HANDY HOLD-UP WILL DISPLAY ARTWORK OR A SPECIAL RECIPE

CHANUKAH HOT PLATE

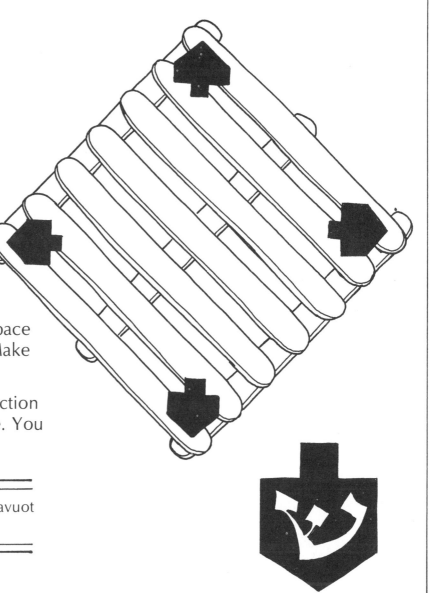

What You Need:

10 popsicle sticks
Construction paper or felt
Scissors, glue, markers

What You Do:

1. Put glue across three popsicle sticks. Space the dry sticks across the three glued ones. Make the ends and edges touch.

2. Cut out Chanukah shapes from construction paper or felt and paste them on the hotplate. You can also decorate it with markers.

TRY THIS TOO: Make hot plates for Pesach and Shavuot with decorations for those holidays.

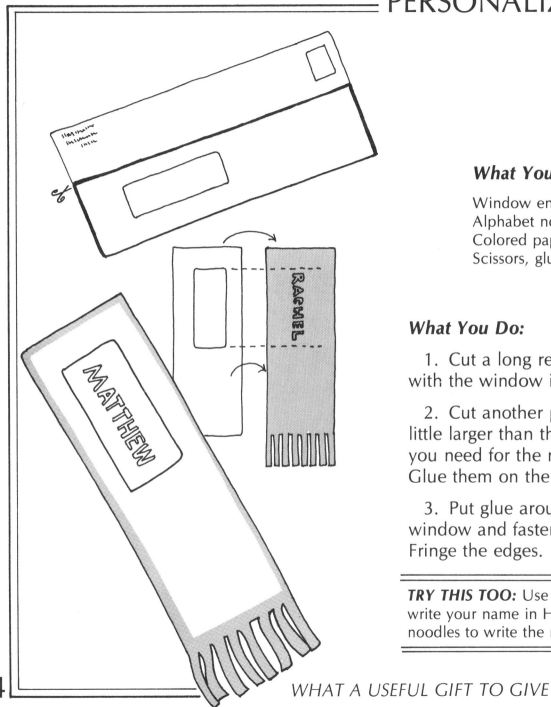

What You Need:

Window envelope (a used one is ok)
Alphabet noodles
Colored paper
Scissors, glue

What You Do:

1. Cut a long rectangle from the envelope with the window in the middle.

2. Cut another piece of colored paper a little larger than the window. Find the letters you need for the name you wish to make. Glue them on the colored paper.

3. Put glue around the edges of the window and fasten it to the colored paper. Fringe the edges.

TRY THIS TOO: Use Hebrew alphabet noodles and write your name in Hebrew. Or use yarn instead of noodles to write the name.

WHAT A USEFUL GIFT TO GIVE

What You Need:

Round can with plastic lid
Colored paper
Plastic flexible straw
Button
Scissors, glue

What You Do:

1. Cover the can with a wide strip of colored paper.

2. Glue the bottom half of the straw to the can. Glue the button to the end of the straw to form the spout.

3. Cut three thin strips of paper. Glue one on each end of the can. Glue the third strip on the side to form a handle.

4. Cut a slit in the plastic lid large enough for coins.

36 *SAVE YOUR COINS TO BUY TREES TO PLANT IN ISRAEL*

FRAME A TREE CERTIFICATE

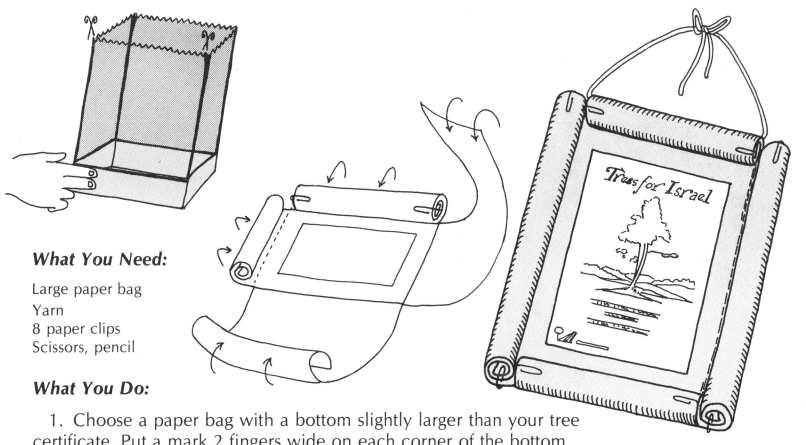

What You Need:

Large paper bag
Yarn
8 paper clips
Scissors, pencil

What You Do:

1. Choose a paper bag with a bottom slightly larger than your tree certificate. Put a mark 2 fingers wide on each corner of the bottom of the bag.

2. Cut down each side to the marks.

3. Roll each cut section tightly as far as you can. Put paper clips on each end to hold the rolls.

4. Glue the tree certificate to the center of the frame.

5. Push yarn through the top roll and tie a loop. The frame is ready to hang!

ISRAEL THANKS YOU FOR PLANTING A TREE

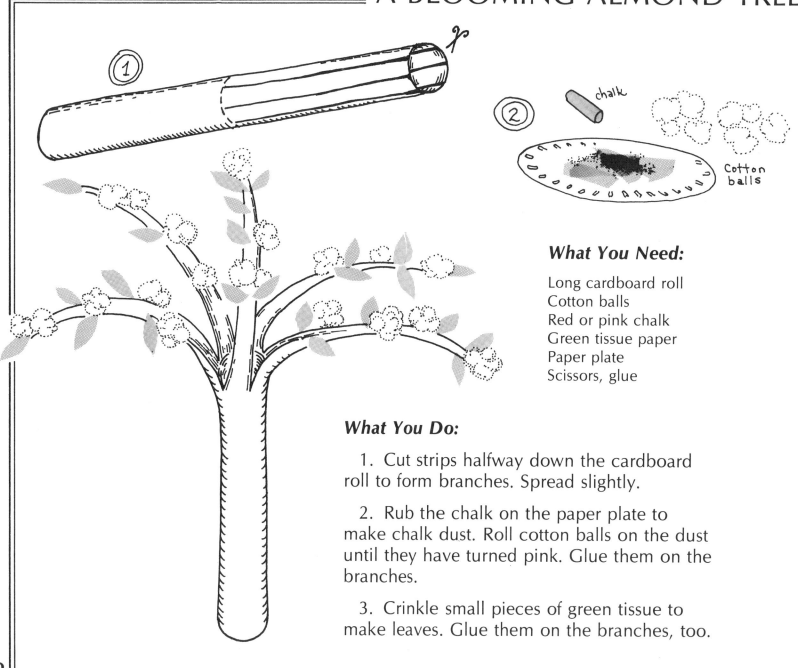

chalk

Cotton balls

What You Need:

Long cardboard roll
Cotton balls
Red or pink chalk
Green tissue paper
Paper plate
Scissors, glue

What You Do:

1. Cut strips halfway down the cardboard roll to form branches. Spread slightly.

2. Rub the chalk on the paper plate to make chalk dust. Roll cotton balls on the dust until they have turned pink. Glue them on the branches.

3. Crinkle small pieces of green tissue to make leaves. Glue them on the branches, too.

IN ISRAEL, THE ALMOND TREE BLOOMS FIRST IN THE SPRING

ORANGE TREE

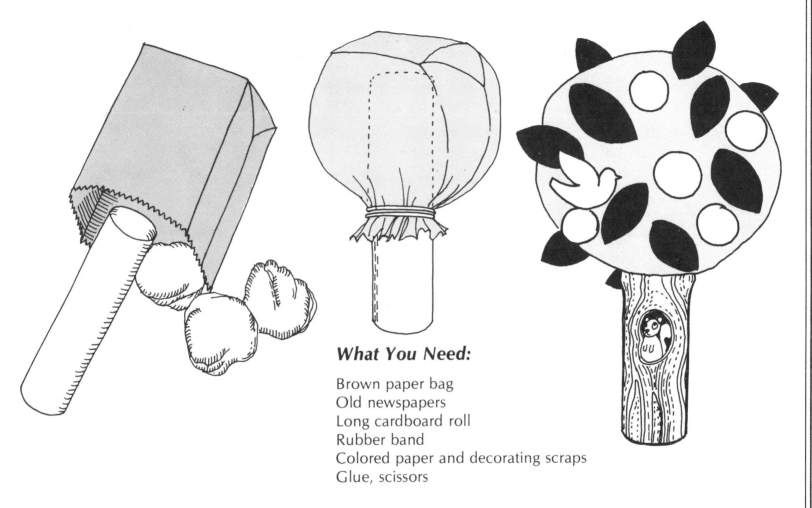

What You Need:

Brown paper bag
Old newspapers
Long cardboard roll
Rubber band
Colored paper and decorating scraps
Glue, scissors

What You Do:

1. Put the cardboard roll in the center of the open paper bag to form a trunk. Crush the newspaper into balls and stuff them all around the trunk.

2. Close the bag around the trunk and fasten with a rubber band.

3. Cover the trunk with dark paper and fabric scraps. Use colorful scraps to decorate the tree with leaves and fruit.

FEED THE WINTER BIRDS

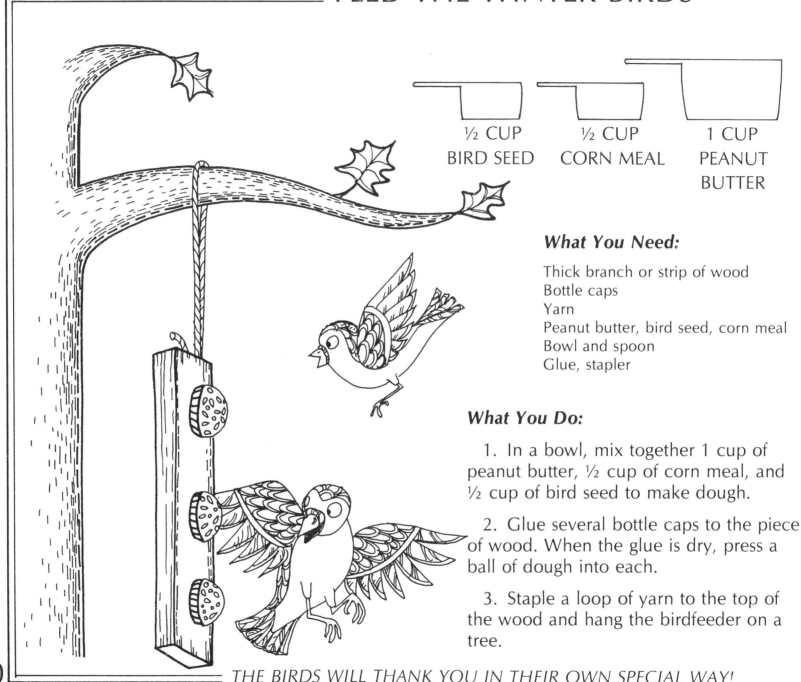

½ CUP
BIRD SEED

½ CUP
CORN MEAL

1 CUP
PEANUT
BUTTER

What You Need:

Thick branch or strip of wood
Bottle caps
Yarn
Peanut butter, bird seed, corn meal
Bowl and spoon
Glue, stapler

What You Do:

1. In a bowl, mix together 1 cup of peanut butter, ½ cup of corn meal, and ½ cup of bird seed to make dough.

2. Glue several bottle caps to the piece of wood. When the glue is dry, press a ball of dough into each.

3. Staple a loop of yarn to the top of the wood and hang the birdfeeder on a tree.

THE BIRDS WILL THANK YOU IN THEIR OWN SPECIAL WAY!

PURIM

HOOT HAMAN

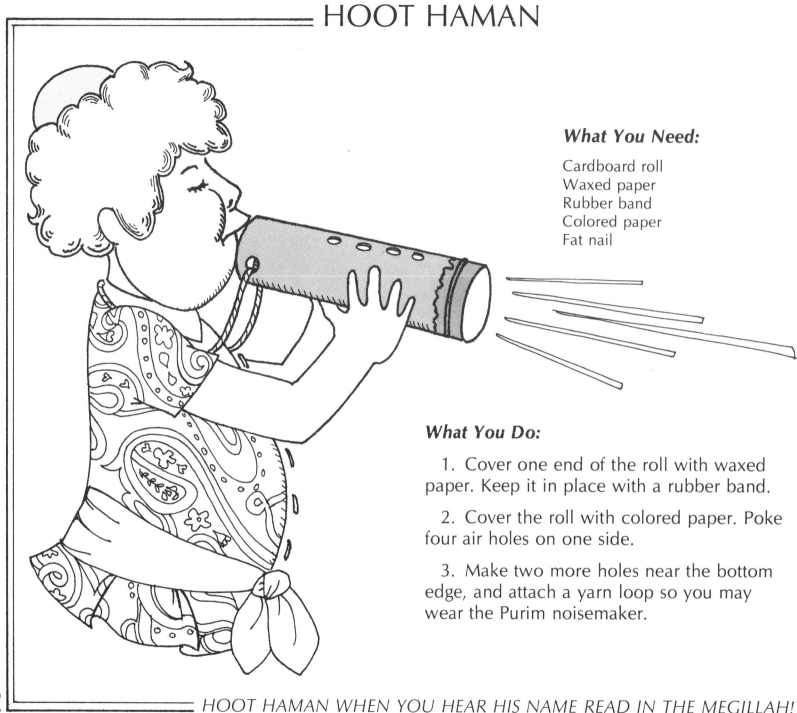

What You Need:

Cardboard roll
Waxed paper
Rubber band
Colored paper
Fat nail

What You Do:

1. Cover one end of the roll with waxed paper. Keep it in place with a rubber band.

2. Cover the roll with colored paper. Poke four air holes on one side.

3. Make two more holes near the bottom edge, and attach a yarn loop so you may wear the Purim noisemaker.

HOOT HAMAN WHEN YOU HEAR HIS NAME READ IN THE MEGILLAH!

JEWELRY FOR QUEEN ESTHER

What You Do:

1. Cut out several small cardboard circles and cover them with foil. Glue pictures of diamonds, rubies, and other jewels on each circle.

2. RING: Punch two small holes in one of the circles, and push the wire fastener through the holes. Shape the ends around your finger and fasten them together to fit.

3. EARRINGS: Punch a hole in two circles. Push through wire fasteners or pipe cleaners long enough to make loops to fit around your ears.

4. NECKLACE: Punch two holes in several circles, and weave them on gold or silver elastic ribbon or a long piece of yarn. Make the necklace long enough to slip over your head easily.

HOW LOVELY YOU ARE, QUEEN ESTHER!

What You Need:

Thin cardboard
Aluminum foil
Wire fastener or pipe cleaner
Pictures of jewelry from magazines
 or catalogs
Elastic ribbon or yarn
Scissors

43

QUICK AND EASY ROBE

What You Need:

Large paper bag
Another paper bag
Paint and paint brush
Yarn
Scissors, glue, stapler
Decorating scraps

What You Do:

1. Cut out the bottom end of a large paper bag. Cut two long narrow strips from another paper bag long enough to fit over your shoulders. Glue or staple the straps to the large paper bag.

2. Paint and decorate the robe. Add a belt made from several long pieces of yarn.

3. Top your costume off with a colorful towel cape!

ANOTHER ROYAL ROBE

What You Need:

Large paper bag
Paint, crayons, markers
Decorating scraps
Pipe cleaners
Scissors, glue, hole punch

What You Do:

1. Cut a line down the center of one of the big sides of the bag from the top to the bottom.

2. Cut a hole out of the bottom of the bag large enough to fit over your head. Try it on to make sure!

3. Cut armholes from each side section of the bag. Try those, too.

4. Punch holes along each of the open sides. Use pipe cleaners to "button up."

5. Decorate your costume with markers and scraps. For Mordecai, be sure to wear a kippah. For Haman, make a cardboard sword to tuck under your belt. For Queen Esther, add a cardboard crown and jewels.

CAN YOUR FRIENDS GUESS WHO YOU ARE?

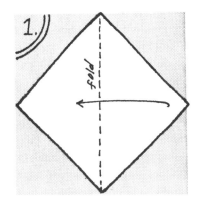

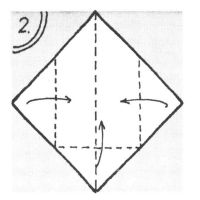

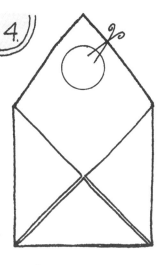

What You Need:

Large paper square
Decorating scraps and
   markers
Scissors, glue, tape

What You Do:

1. Turn the paper square so it looks like a diamond. Fold the diamond in half sideways and unfold it.

2. Fold each side to the center fold. Fold the bottom point up to meet the side points. Glue or tape them together.

3. Decorate the basket with scraps, and write TO, FROM, and a Purim greeting.

4. Cut out a hole near the top point. If your friends are away when you arrive, you may hang the basket on the doorknob.

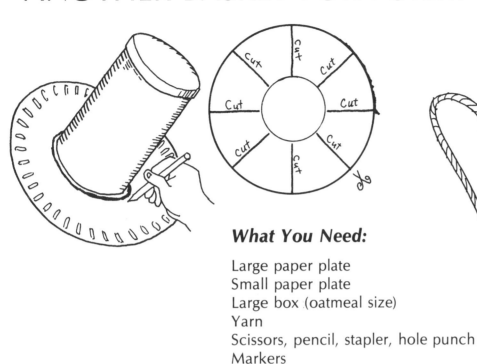

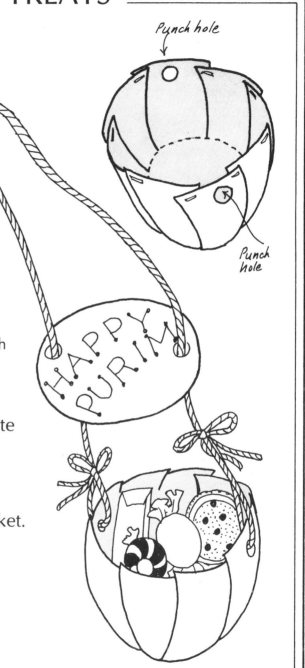

What You Need:

Large paper plate
Small paper plate
Large box (oatmeal size)
Yarn
Scissors, pencil, stapler, hole punch
Markers

What You Do:

1. Put the oatmeal box in the center of the large plate and trace around it. Cut eight evenly spaced slits from the outside rim into the center circle.

2. Overlap each of the cut sections and staple them together. Punch two holes in opposite sides of the basket.

3. Write HAPPY PURIM on top of the small paper plate. Make two holes on opposite sides of it.

4. Tie one end of a long piece of yarn to the basket. Push it through one hole in the lid, pull it across, and push it down through holes in the lid and basket.

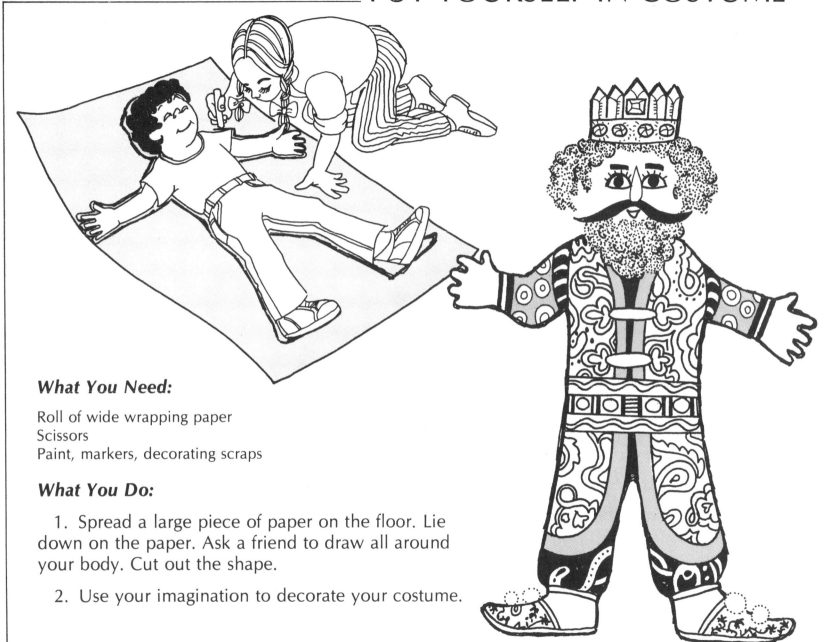

What You Need:

Roll of wide wrapping paper
Scissors
Paint, markers, decorating scraps

What You Do:

1. Spread a large piece of paper on the floor. Lie down on the paper. Ask a friend to draw all around your body. Cut out the shape.

2. Use your imagination to decorate your costume.

CAN YOUR FRIENDS GUESS THAT IT'S REALLY YOU?

PESACH

FORSYTHIA FLOWERS FOR THE SEDER TABLE

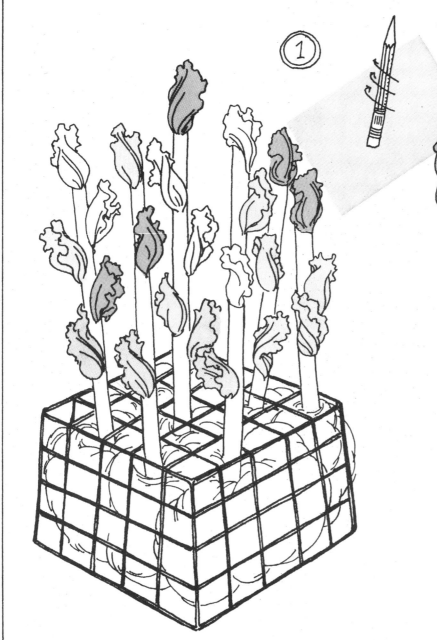

What You Need:

Plastic box from fruits or vegetables
Two paper napkins
Yellow tissue paper
Plastic straws
Jar lid
Pencil, scissors, glue

What You Do:

1. Cut small squares of tissue. Place the eraser end of a pencil in the center of each square, and twist the paper around the pencil.

2. Pour a small amount of glue in the jar lid. Dip the tissue covered pencil into the glue, then stick it on top of a plastic straw and carefully remove the pencil.

3. Fluff the napkins into balls, and stuff them in the vegetable box.

4. Turn the box over, and push the straws through the holes in the box so the flowers will stand in the vase.

FORSYTHIA IS ONE OF THE FIRST FLOWERS TO BLOOM IN THE SPRING!

COLORFUL KIPPAH

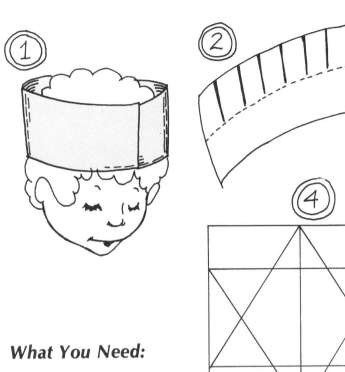

What You Need:

Colored paper
Glue, scissors

What You Do:

1. Make a wide headband from a long piece of colored paper.

2. Cut twelve evenly spaced slits around the top of the headband. Glue each tab over the one next to it.

3. Cut out a Jewish star from a different colored paper. Glue it down to cover the top of the crown.

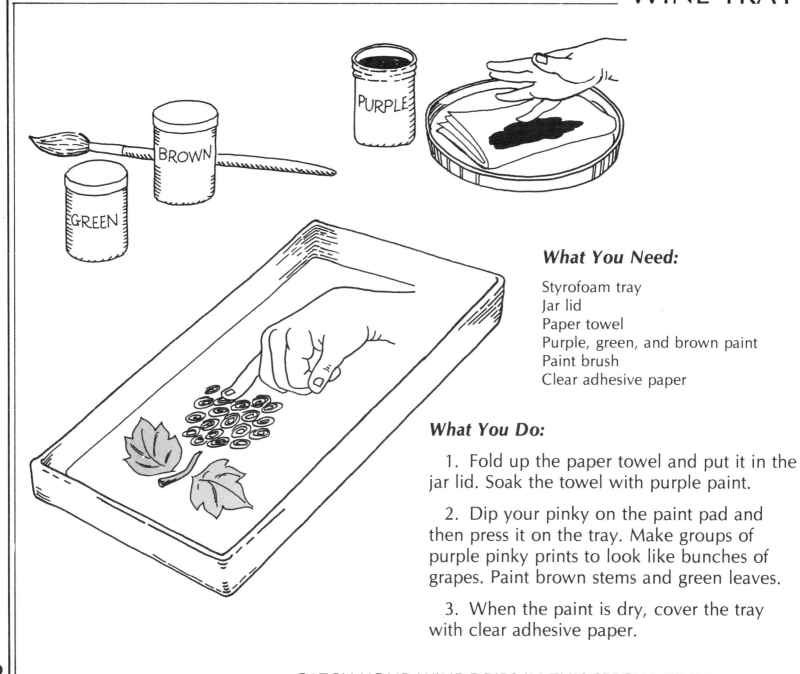

What You Need:

Styrofoam tray
Jar lid
Paper towel
Purple, green, and brown paint
Paint brush
Clear adhesive paper

What You Do:

1. Fold up the paper towel and put it in the jar lid. Soak the towel with purple paint.

2. Dip your pinky on the paint pad and then press it on the tray. Make groups of purple pinky prints to look like bunches of grapes. Paint brown stems and green leaves.

3. When the paint is dry, cover the tray with clear adhesive paper.

CATCH YOUR WINE DRIPS IN THIS SPECIAL TRAY

MATZAH TRAY

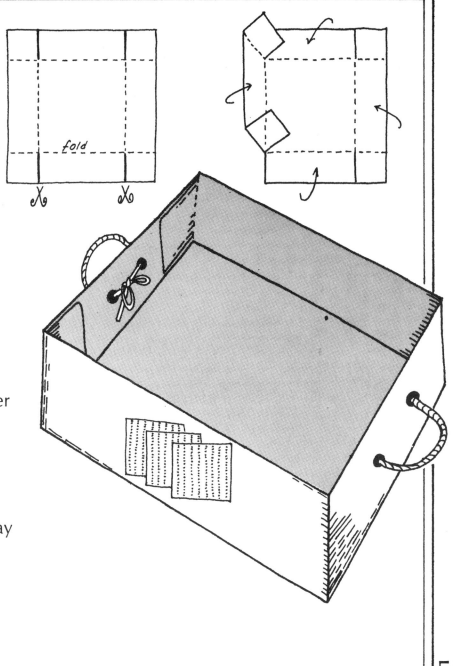

What You Need:

12-inch square of heavy paper
Strong yarn or pipe cleaners
Glue, pencil, hole punch
Brown crayon or marker
White drawing paper

What You Do:

1. Place a box of matzah in the middle of the paper and trace around it. Turn the paper over so the lines are on the bottom. Fold up the sides to the lines.

2. Cut one slit up to the fold line at each corner. Glue the side flaps inside.

3. Punch two holes on two sides of the tray and attach yarn or pipe cleaners to make handles.

4. Draw and cut out small squares of paper. Decorate them to look like matzot, and glue them to the sides of the tray.

USE YOUR MATZAH TRAY ALL OF PESACH

SEDER PILLOW

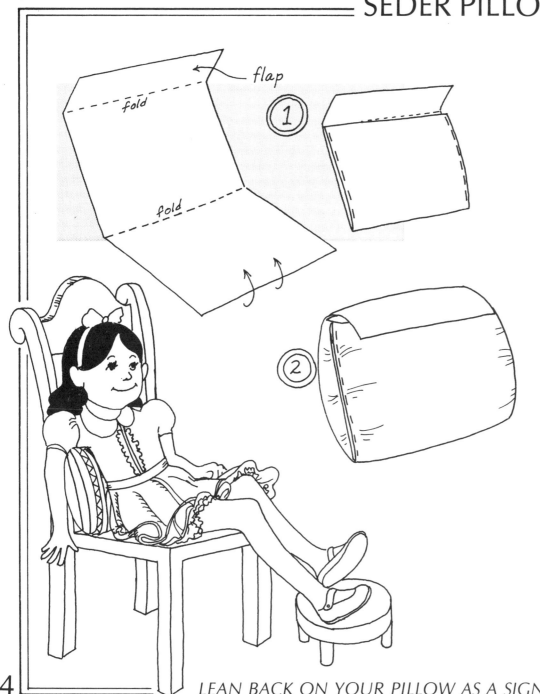

flap

fold

fold

①

②

What You Need:

Long rectangle of strong white paper (shelf paper or cut-up grocery bag)
Old newspapers
Colored paper
Scissors, glue, markers

What You Do:

1. Fold the paper rectangle almost in half, leaving a short flap on one end. Staple the sides closed.

2. Crumple up newspaper balls and stuff them inside to make a fat pillow. Put glue on the flap and fold it down to close the pillow. Glue a folded strip of colored paper along each side to cover the staples.

3. Decorate with markers and colored paper shapes.

LEAN BACK ON YOUR PILLOW AS A SIGN OF A FREE PERSON

FOUR CUP COUNTER

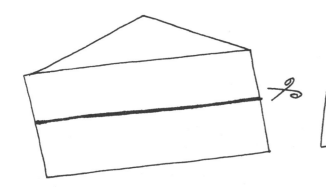

What You Need:

Used envelope
Colored paper
Scissors, colored markers

What You Do:

1. Cut a strip from the bottom of the envelope. Open the ends and flatten them out. This will make a triangle pocket at each end. Fold over one end, so there is a pocket in front and one in back.

2. Cut out shapes of four small cups of wine. Put them in the front pocket. Make a pretty design on the rest of the marker.

3. After you drink each cup of wine at the seder, move one paper wine cup from the front to the hidden back pocket.

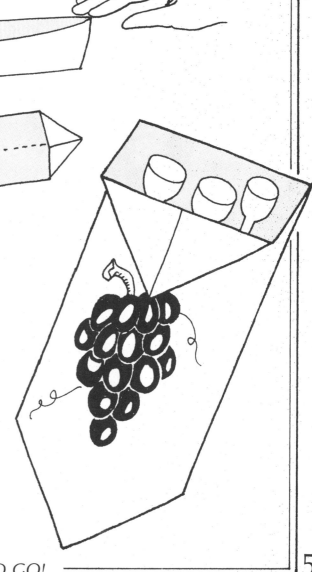

NOW YOU CAN COUNT HOW MANY MORE TO GO!

What You Need:

Thin cardboard
Brown crayon or marker
Scissors, glue

What You Do:

1. Draw a design of three seder matzot and cut it out. Color it. Cut a slit in the middle matzah.

2. To mark your place, push the page corner through the slit.

56

A "NO HANDS" SEDER GAME

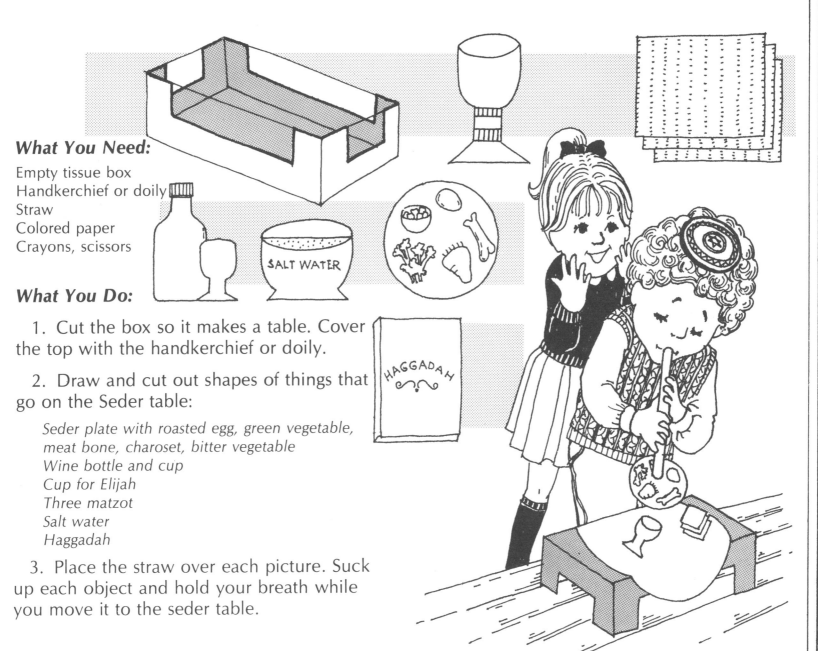

What You Need:

Empty tissue box
Handkerchief or doily
Straw
Colored paper
Crayons, scissors

What You Do:

1. Cut the box so it makes a table. Cover the top with the handkerchief or doily.

2. Draw and cut out shapes of things that go on the Seder table:

   Seder plate with roasted egg, green vegetable, meat bone, charoset, bitter vegetable
   Wine bottle and cup
   Cup for Elijah
   Three matzot
   Salt water
   Haggadah

3. Place the straw over each picture. Suck up each object and hold your breath while you move it to the seder table.

WHAT A FUN WAY TO SET THE TABLE!

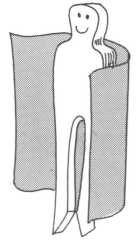

What You Need:

Egg carton lid
Aluminum foil
Cotton
Fabric
Clothespin
Scissors, glue, markers

What You Do:

1. Cut the egg carton lid in half. Cover it with aluminum foil. Build the foil up along with cut side, so that it is even with the other sides.

2. Glue cotton balls to line the inside of the lid.

3. Cut fabric to fit inside the lid. Put glue along the sides and gently press the blanket fabric on the cotton lining.

4. Use the clothespin for Baby Moses. Draw his face with a marker. Tuck him under the blanket.

BABY MOSES CAN FLOAT IN YOUR BATHTUB!

YOM HA'ATZMAUT

WALK-A-THON BACKSACK

fold

2 folds

What You Need:

Medium size paper bag
Two old neckties or strong yarn
Colored paper
Scissors, markers, and glue

What You Do:

1. Open the paper bag. Fold over a flap all around the top. Now fold it over again.

2. On one wide side of the bag, cut two small holes on the flap near each corner and two small holes below them near the bottom corners. Push an old necktie or heavy yarn through each pair of holes. Tie the ends together so the backsack fits you.

3. Decorate the sack with special designs for Israel's birthday.

WHAT WILL YOU TUCK IN YOUR SACK? HOW ABOUT A SNACK!

BIRTHDAY FAN FOR ISRAEL

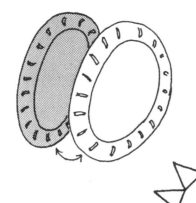

What You Need:

2 paper plates
Large cardboard roll
Old magazine or colored paper
Scissors, glue, markers

What You Do:

1. Glue the rims of the paper plates together, front to front.

2. Cut two deep slits in the cardboard roll. Push the plate into the slits. Put glue along the slits to hold the plates tight.

3. Cut out big letters I S R A E L from a magazine, or make them from colored paper. Glue them on one side of the fan. Glue Israel's birthday numbers on the other side.

4. Draw colorful balloon shapes around each letter and number. Draw wiggly strings from each balloon to the fan handle.

KEEP COOL WHILE YOU WALK IN ISRAEL'S BIRTHDAY PARADE

What You Need:

½ cup applesauce

1¼ cups water

1½ tablespoons honey

⅓ cup powdered milk

1 tablespoon baking soda

Plastic jar with lid

What You Do:

1. Put all ingredients except baking soda in the jar. Cover with the lid and shake, shake, shake.

2. Add the baking soda and shake some more. The baking soda will make the milkshake fizzy and frothy.

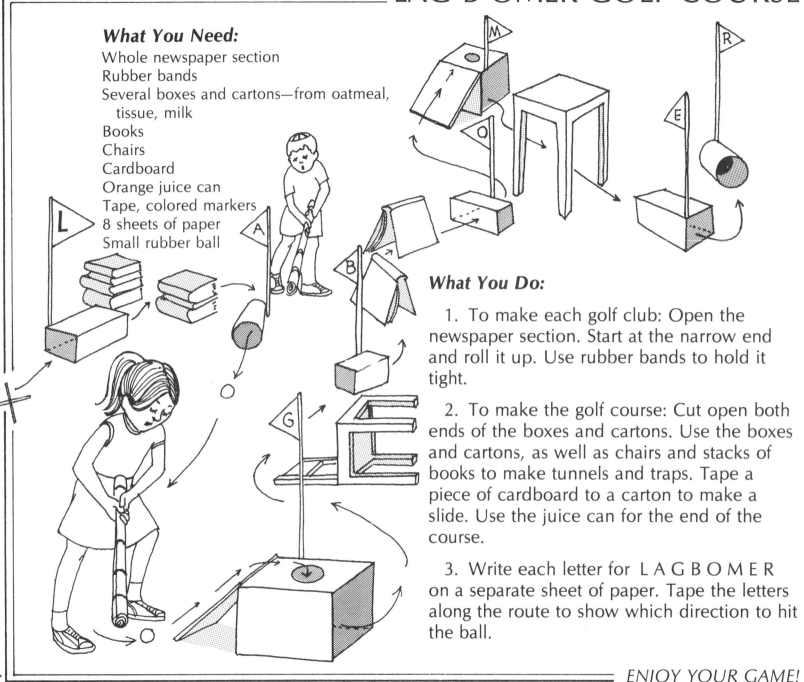

What You Need:

Whole newspaper section
Rubber bands
Several boxes and cartons—from oatmeal, tissue, milk
Books
Chairs
Cardboard
Orange juice can
Tape, colored markers
8 sheets of paper
Small rubber ball

What You Do:

1. To make each golf club: Open the newspaper section. Start at the narrow end and roll it up. Use rubber bands to hold it tight.

2. To make the golf course: Cut open both ends of the boxes and cartons. Use the boxes and cartons, as well as chairs and stacks of books to make tunnels and traps. Tape a piece of cardboard to a carton to make a slide. Use the juice can for the end of the course.

3. Write each letter for L A G B O M E R on a separate sheet of paper. Tape the letters along the route to show which direction to hit the ball.

SHOE PUPPET

back

front

What You Need:

A shoe
Construction paper
Scissors, markers, glue
Decorating scraps

What You Do:

1. Draw around your shoe print. Cut it out.

2. Cut out paper arms and legs, and glue them to the shoe body.

3. Add clothing, hair, and other decorations.

MAKE SHOE PUPPETS FOR OTHER HOLIDAYS, TOO!

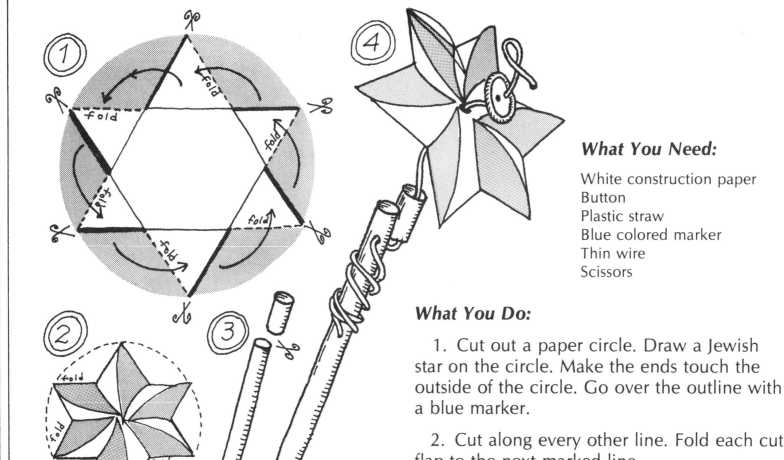

What You Need:

White construction paper
Button
Plastic straw
Blue colored marker
Thin wire
Scissors

What You Do:

1. Cut out a paper circle. Draw a Jewish star on the circle. Make the ends touch the outside of the circle. Go over the outline with a blue marker.

2. Cut along every other line. Fold each cut flap to the next marked line.

3. Cut a short slice off one end of the straw.

4. Loop a piece of wire through the button, push it through the middle of the star, through the short piece of straw and through the long straw. Twist the wire around the straw to fasten it.

AN EXTRA PICNIC POCKET

What You Need:

2 small paper plates
Colored tissue paper
Containers of water
Yarn
Paint brush
Hole punch, stapler

What You Do:

1. Cut a slice off of one side of a paper plate. Staple the cut plate to the uncut plate, front to front.

2. To decorate the pocket, put a small piece of colored tissue on the cut plate. Dip the paintbrush in water and wet the entire tissue. Lift up the tissue. SURPRISE! The color of the tissue went onto the plate. Repeat with different colored tissue scraps to make a design all over the plates.

3. Punch a hole near the top of the uncut plate. Attach a piece of yarn, so you may wear the pocket around your neck or tied to your waist.

YOUR POCKET CAN HOLD ROCKS, LEAVES, SEEDS, AND OTHER TREASURES

BLOW COLORED BUBBLES

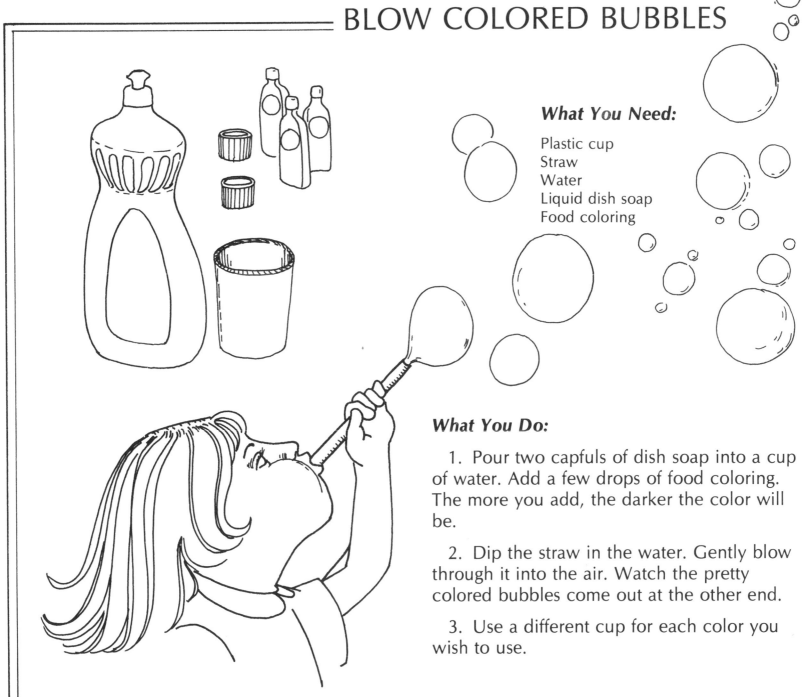

What You Need:

Plastic cup
Straw
Water
Liquid dish soap
Food coloring

What You Do:

1. Pour two capfuls of dish soap into a cup of water. Add a few drops of food coloring. The more you add, the darker the color will be.

2. Dip the straw in the water. Gently blow through it into the air. Watch the pretty colored bubbles come out at the other end.

3. Use a different cup for each color you wish to use.

WATCH THE BREEZE CARRY YOUR BUBBLES TO THE SKY

SHAVUOT

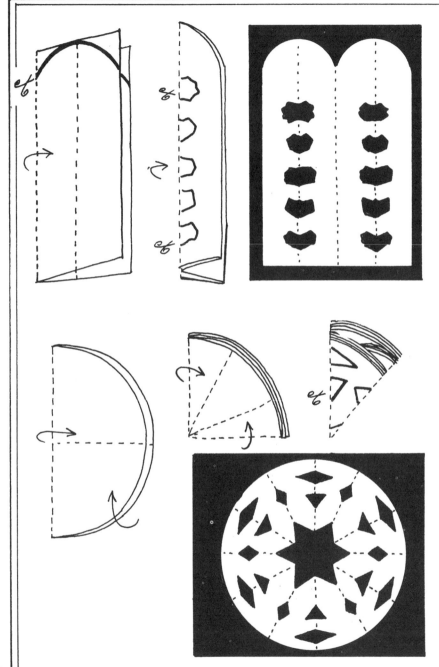

What You Need:

Colored paper
White paper
Scissors, glue

What You Do:

1. To make the Ten Commandments:
Fold a piece of white paper in half. Cut
a curve along the top two edges. Fold
the paper in half again. Cut five shapes
on the long folded side. Unfold and
glue the papercut onto colored paper.

2. To make a Star of David design:
Fold a circle of white paper in half and
in half again. Then fold in each side to
make an ice cream cone shape. Cut off
the bottom point with a slanted line.
Cut out shapes along the folds on each
side and along the top. Unfold and glue
the papercut onto colored paper.

MAKE SEVERAL PAPERCUTS TO DECORATE YOUR HOME AND SCHOOL

BASKET FOR SHAVUOT GREENS

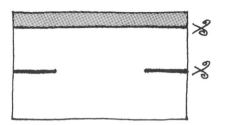

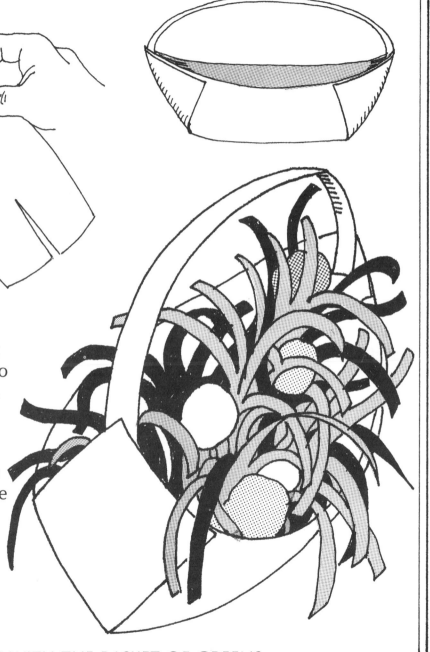

What You Need:

Construction paper
Tissue paper
Scissors, glue, markers

What You Do:

1. Cut a narrow strip off the long side of the paper to make a handle. Cut a line along the center of each short side. Overlap the two ends and fasten with glue. Attach the handle.

2. Cut out Shavuot greens from dark and light green paper. Fringe some to look like grass. Crumble tissue paper to look like some of the first fruits harvested. Glue them into the basket of greens.

DECORATE THE SHAVUOT HOLIDAY TABLE WITH THE BASKET OF GREENS

What You Need:

Construction paper
Brad fastener
Blue and white yarn
Scissors, glue

What You Do:

1. Measure a long strip of paper to fit your head. Glue the ends together. Cut slits one third of the way down all around the top of the headband. Fold the flaps down.

2. Cut a square of paper larger than the headband. Put glue on the flaps of the headband and press them onto the paper square.

3. Make a tassle with blue and white yarn and fasten it to the center of the square.

WEAR YOUR CAP WHEN YOU LEARN A NEW BLESSING OR SONG